Children
Everywhere

by David L. Harrison

illustrated by Gordon Laite

RAND McNALLY & COMPANY Chicago / New York / San Francisco

Library of Congress Cataloging in Publication Data
Harrison, David Lee, 1937-
    Children everywhere.

    SUMMARY: Twelve children throughout the world
describe their lives—the foods they eat, the games
they play, and the chores they perform.
    1. Manners and customs—Juvenile literature.
2. Children in foreign countries—Juvenile literature.
[1. Manners and customs.   2. Children in foreign
countries]   I. Laite, Gordon, illus.   II. Title.
GT85.H37 1973   390   73-7651
ISBN 0-528-82164-4
ISBN 0-528-82165-2 (lib. bdg.)

First printing 1973

Contents

Around the World

Utak lives in a house of snow.

Martta's house is made of cloth.

Putu lives in a house of bamboo, and each room is a separate little house.

Toma sometimes uses a piece of bark for a plate.

Chen-fu eats with chopsticks.

Mendak scoops up his rice with bread.

And Rifa'a eats with her fingers.

Around the world, children live in many different kinds of houses. They use different kinds of things in their daily lives. And yet, though different from one another in many ways, children everywhere are sometimes very much alike.

Kites flutter above islands, deserts, mountaintops, and valleys. Sleds slide across snow, sand, cobblestones, and ice. Boys and girls around the world like to sing, hear stories, help their mothers and fathers, and collect all sorts of animals to love.

Children everywhere do the things that only children like to do!

Utak

The Arctic

Norway

Robin

United States

NORTH
AMERICA

EUR

France

Mexico

Françoise

AFRICA

Pablo

SOUTH
AMERICA

Brazil

Toma

Ronaldo

Martta

Chen-fu

ASIA

China

Saudi
Arabia

India

Putu

Rifa'a

Bali

Mendak

AUSTRALIA

Ian

Utak from the Arctic

Dogsled

Bone Fishhook with Sinew
Line and Reel of Antler

Box Made of Ice
for Storing Fish

My name is Utak, and I welcome you to the Arctic. We Eskimos don't often have visitors.

Up here the winter days grow shorter and shorter. Finally a day comes in December when there is no sunlight at all. For many weeks it is dark all day and all night until at last the sun again peeps over the edge of the sky. So if you spend the winter night with an Eskimo you have lots of time to play.

During the long winter night my family travels by dogsled to a place where white Arctic foxes live. With his knife my father cuts big blocks of snow. Then he builds us a snow house called an igloo. A thin sheet of ice makes a windowpane.

Inside we shape a bed of snow and cover it with caribou skins and sleeping robes. Burning oil from seal fat keeps our snow home snug and warm.

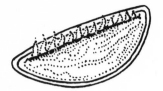

Seal-Fat Burner

Ulu

Kakivak

Drum

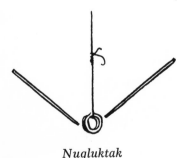

Nugluktak

Arctic winters are so cold that even the ocean freezes over. To keep warm I wear a caribou-skin shirt, polar-bear-skin pants, and sealskin boots. Wolverine fur lines my parka hood and hare fur lines my mittens.

Each day my father harnesses our nine huskies to the sled and rides out to see if his traps have caught any foxes. Sometimes he takes me fishing, or we hunt caribou, seals, or hare.

My spear, called a *kakivak*, has sharp points made from caribou horn. I use it to spear fish through holes in the ice. In the cold air the fish freeze and become so stiff that I can stand them on their tails.

Sometimes we cook our meat. But when it's frozen we like it better raw. When we eat meat we hold one end of it between our teeth and slice off a bite with a sharp knife called an *ulu*. Once my uncle Jakupi's *ulu* slipped and clipped off the tip of his nose.

Even in the dark winter I still like to play outside. It's fun to zip across the ice on the sled my father made from a strip of frozen whale skin. I play my drum too. My uncle Kayak made it by stretching caribou hide over a wooden hoop.

At night we may play *nugluktak*. That's an old Eskimo game in which everyone tries to poke sticks through a bone ring hanging from the ceiling. It's hard to hit that little hole when it begins to dance and spin.

Toward spring the sun will return to the sky. The weather will turn warmer and we will go home to sell our fox furs. Our house in the village has a kitchen and a bedroom. In it we have furniture and electric lights and a big stove.

But I'm always glad when winter comes again. Then we follow the trail of the Arctic fox and live far out on the ice in our snug little igloo of snow.

Putu from Bali

Putu's Bird in Its Cage

Putu's House

Ah, it is morning! Roosters are crowing and dogs are barking. In her cage near my bed my dove sings her morning song.

My name is Putu and I live on the island of Bali in the Pacific Ocean. Join me for breakfast and I'll show you my home. Do you like milk and cake? Good! It's coconut milk and rice cake. We eat with our right hands and use palm leaves for plates.

All the rooms in my home are separate little houses. The kitchen is one little house. So is the room where we children sleep. Our room has no walls, so the ocean breezes keep us cool. The coconut-leaf room keeps us dry. My bed is made of bamboo and is covered with a thick mat. Around our yard runs a mud-brick wall, and inside it are flocks of ducks and chickens and the biggest, fattest pigs you ever saw.

One of the piglets is mine. Every morning I gather weeds and leaves and boil them for him in a kettle on the stove. When he grows fat enough I will sell him and save the money.

16

After breakfast my brother Popol and I herd the ducks out to our rice fields, where they look for food. On my head I carry a coconut shell filled with cool water for my father to drink while he works. When I was first learning to carry the shells, I often spilled the water and got a cold shower I didn't expect!

Dragonflies dart about the fields and sun themselves on the rice plants. Popol and I use twigs dipped in sticky sap to capture them. Sometimes at night we use long wooden pincers to catch the small eels that live in the water. Dragonflies and eels taste delicious cooked with rice.

In the afternoon Popol likes to fly the kite that our father made for him. It's much bigger than he is and looks like a giant bird dipping and diving across the sky.

What I like most is to dance. In Bali young girls make the best dancers. I've been taking lessons since I was three years old. When I'm thirteen I will begin teaching younger girls.

Tomorrow is a festival day and I will dance in the temple. Tonight my mother has set out the bright robes of green and red that I will wear. Early in the morning fresh flowers must be picked for my golden headpiece.

Now the tiny night lizards are chirping their lullaby. Soon they will sing me to sleep until my dove calls me in the morning.

Good night! I'm glad you came to see me.

Dragonflies

Rice Plants

Flowers for Putu's Headdress

Popol's Kite

Pablo from Mexico

Clay Animals and Jar

Tortillas and Taco

Banana Tree

Buenos días! I, Pablo, welcome you to Mexico. You have come at a good time. Tomorrow is a fiesta day in our village, and there is much excitement in my family.

All morning my mother has prepared food. First she ground corn kernels into meal. From this she made thin, round cakes called tortillas, which she roasted on our metal stove. She will fold some of the tortillas and fill them with meat, goat cheese, beans, hot sauce, and lettuce to make tacos.

My sister María filled a jar with cool water at the village fountain. She put flowers on the table and swept the concrete floor well. Then she washed our clothes in the river. We will look fresh tomorrow.

My brothers, Benito and Juan, and I helped our father. We loaded the wooden cart with his little clay animals to sell at the fiesta.

Someday I will be a potter like my father. Already some of my clay vases have been sold in the market. I decorate mine with triangles, but my father paints fancy roosters and cows on his.

Our house is also built of clay, which we mixed with straw and water and shaped into bricks. In the back is a shady patio. Our chickens take cool dust baths there while our turkey pecks for food. At night we shut the cow and burro inside the courtyard. Then they come to the patio too.

21

Burro with Carrying Baskets

Serape for Pablo's Father

Tonight I will lie on my straw mat and think of the fiesta. Early in the morning the church bells will bong and clang. The cobblestone streets will ring with the clip-clopping hooves of burros pulling loaded carts.

All along the streets people will sell good things to eat. I can almost smell the bubbling pots of soup, the heaping platters of roast pork and chicken, and the juicy slices of red watermelon. I always buy a stalk of sugarcane to chew on while I explore.

Soon the fireworks will begin. Then it sounds like all the balloons in the world are popping all over town. Musicians playing trumpets, violins, and guitars will stroll here and there while people sing and shout and dance in the streets.

If we sell enough clay animals perhaps our father will buy us wooden masks or toy bulls made of straw. María likes cloth dolls. Maybe we will even ride the merry-go-round and the Ferris wheel.

The afternoon will be filled with horse races and cockfights and bullfights. After dark there will be puppet shows. The fun will last all day and far into the night.

When at last we start home, the stars will twinkle like sparklers and the moon will sit high in the sky. Then I will nod and lean against my father and sleep as the cart bumps along.

I hope that someday you can see a fiesta with me. Pablo will show you a good time. *Buenas noches!*

Cart

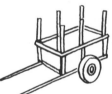

Firecrackers

Sombrero

Françoise from France

Roller Skates

Françoise's Doll

Narcissus Bulbs in Bowl

Bonjour! My name is Françoise, and I live in France in the city of Tours.

Would you like to go to the river this afternoon? The Loire River runs through Tours, and my grandfather sometimes takes me with him when he goes to fish from the bank. It is very pleasant to pack a picnic basket and ride our bicycles to the river. I carry his fishing pole over my shoulder.

Before we go I'll show you my room, which is upstairs at the front of the house. On the dresser I keep a wooden sailboat that my father made for my birthday. On Sundays I take my boat to the park and enter the races held on the pond there. Last Sunday I finished second, and my parents bought me a gingerbread pig with my name written in frosting on it. I'm keeping it beside my boat.

Hanging from my bedpost is one of my favorite toys. It's a clown puppet with strings that make him dance and jump when I wiggle my fingers. I also have a doll, which I keep in a doll carriage near the window.

On my wall are a map of France and a picture of the ocean where my family went last summer for vacation. What fun that was! I still have the beach ball we played with in the sand. It reminds me of the good times we had.

Are you hungry? Then you must stay for lunch. Every morning my mother sends me to the baker's with money to buy fresh bread. The loaves are half as long as I am and they stick out across the back of my bicycle as I pedal home.

By the time I reach the kitchen, good smells are coming from the pots and pans bubbling on the stove. Today we are having mashed potatoes, boiled cabbage, horse liver, and thick slices of the crusty bread. For dessert there will be fruit and cheese.

My best friend is a girl named Cécile, who lives next door. When we have enough money we each buy a big bright balloon and tie it on a long string. We have to be careful around Pierre though. He's my pet cat and he loves to pounce on balloons!

In the evenings after dinner I help my mother wash the dishes while we listen to the radio. During the summer my father pulls the weeds in his garden. Before bedtime I like to read a story while my mother sews and my father plays his concertina. Right now he's making me a new boat to race in the park.

Early in the morning Pierre will pad up the stairs to my room. He'll meow to let me know that it's time for his milk and my bread and jam. That's a nice way to start a new day, don't you think?

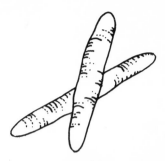

French Bread

Pierre

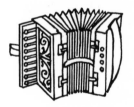

Concertina

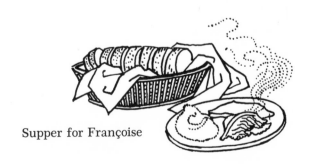

Supper for Françoise

Toma from Africa

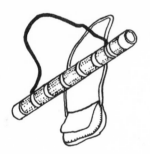

Pouch and Quiver
to Hold Arrows

Tsama Melon Pot

Hello! My name is Toma, and I'm a Bushman boy. I'm happy that you have come to Africa to visit me.

My house is made of branches stuck into the ground and covered with grass. It has no door or floor. We don't need a big house because we live outdoors. But on cold nights, as we sleep on the ground, our little house helps keep us warm.

When I wake up each day I eat by the fire in front of our house. This morning my sister Twikwe and I shared a juicy melon called a tsama. Tsama melon shells are so hard that my mother uses them for cooking pots. My father stretched antelope skin over one and made me a drum.

After the morning meal the men go hunting. Sometimes they set traps for warthogs or anteaters or ostriches. Sometimes they hunt for antelope or giraffes with their poison-tipped arrows. I'm not old enough to hunt. But when my father rubs poison on his arrows, he lets me dry them by the fire.

Ostrich

Ostrich Eggs

Ostrich-Shell Beads
and Bracelet

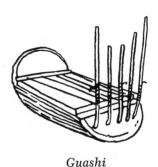

Guashi

After the men leave camp, the women and children gather firewood and things to eat. I like to dig with a sharp stick for ga roots. Ga roots are big and brown and warty, but they taste good when they're cooked.

Water is hard to find in our part of Africa. When we travel we carry water with us in ostrich eggshells. Sometimes we bury extra eggshells along the way. Then if the water holes all dry up we still have something to drink.

When an eggshell breaks the women make necklaces and strings of beads with the pieces. Twikwe wears beads in her hair. Boys don't wear things like that. But I do wear a leather band around my arm. My father made it of antelope skin. It's supposed to bring me luck.

Late in the day everyone returns to camp for the evening meal. Last night my mother baked a tortoise I caught. She stuffed it with green leaves, wild onions, and mushrooms. We used pieces of bark for plates and ate with our fingers. Hmmmmm! It tasted nearly as good as roasted termites!

After supper our father pulled Twikwe and me around camp on an old cape of antelope skin. Our mother watched and played music on her *guashi*. A *guashi* is made from a hollow log and has five strings to strum.

Sometimes at night our people tie cocoon rattles to their ankles and dance and sing around the campfires under the stars. We believe that the stars are hunters like us who must move across the sky forever looking for food.

Now it is time to sleep. Far off in the night I hear a lion roaring. He's getting up and I'm going to bed. Good night! Come back soon!

Martta from Norway

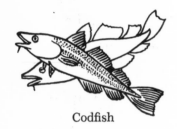

Codfish

Martta's Summer Shoes

Cradle

Have you ever slept in a tent? You could if you stayed with me this summer in Norway.

My name is Martta and my people are called Lapps. We live in the Far North, where winters are long and dark and cold. But summers are warm and the sun shines all day and all night. At the first sign of summer we leave our log house and move our reindeer herd to the green pastures near the ocean.

In the summer we live in a tent made of birch-tree poles covered with heavy cloth. In the middle of the tent we build a stone fireplace. A heavy cooking pot hangs over it on a chain from the ceiling. Reindeer hides cover the floor, and a hole at the top lets smoke out. When my father brings home a big fish from the ocean, he hangs it in the smoke near the ceiling for a few days. Then my mother makes soup.

My mother is a good cook and I'm learning too. She can bake cakes using wild-bird eggs and make pies filled with little fish. Sometimes I fix our breakfast of fish eggs and fresh blueberries.

After meals I sweep the fireplace with a broom made from swan wings. Then I clean our wooden spoons and bowls and the cooking pots by wiping them with hay dipped in water.

Martta's Doll

Carved Antler Spoons

When that's done I like to take my dog, Gargo, and go play. Yesterday we found a bird with a hurt wing and I brought it home. I will take care of it until it can fly again.

Later I feed my baby goat, Siri, and milk my reindeer, Berit. Reindeer are important to Lapps. They give us milk and meat. Their hides make warm robes and beds. From their antlers we carve spoons and knives and tools.

On days when my friend Rist comes over, we play with my dolls. My father carved them from wood and my mother sewed clothes for them. They look just like little Lapp girls.

If Rist's brother Turi comes, we play ball or Hide-and-Seek or Blindman's Buff. Sometimes he ties reindeer horns on his head and we try to lasso him.

At night my mother and father tell me stories about animals and magicians and bear hunts. When the fire burns low I lie on my reindeer-hide bed with a bundle under my head and a thick, warm rug for a quilt. Softly I sing songs that our people have sung for as long as anyone can remember.

And before I go to sleep I think how glad I am to be a Lapp girl.

Martta's Winter House

Ronaldo from Brazil

Leaves and Blossoms
of Coffee Tree

Coffee Cherries

Two Beans Inside
Coffee Cherry

Basketful of
Coffee Cherries

Welcome to Brazil! My name is Ronaldo, and I live on a coffee plantation. Come out on the porch where it is shady and swing in my hammock. I will climb a carambola tree and pick some juicy yellow fruit for a snack. Then we can hitch a horse to a cart and I'll show you around our plantation.

We have thousands of coffee trees. In the spring the air is sweet with their snowy blossoms. In the summer their branches droop with rich red cherries. Our whole family works to pick the cherries and spread them in the sun to dry.

Nestled inside each cherry are two green coffee beans. My father takes the beans to market where they are loaded on ships and carried to many other countries. Maybe your mother has some of our good-smelling coffee in your kitchen.

One of my favorite places on the plantation is the horse shed. On rainy days I hunt mice there with my slingshot, but they're usually too quick for me to hit.

On breezy days I like to fly kites with my brother Antonio. My newest one is made of cloth cut in the shape of a bird and is as brightly colored as a parrot.

37

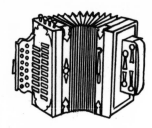

Ronaldo's Accordion

Ronaldo's Hammock

Fan

Painted Gourd Cup

Telma's Guitar

I have a real parrot too. His name is José and he talks all the time. He thinks it's a good joke to whistle and call my dog. Everyone laughs and thinks it's funny. But my dog doesn't think it's funny at all.

José came from another part of Brazil. So did many other things in our home. My mother has a fruit basket made of straw and a lace scarf woven with thread made from banana leaves. My father's rocking chair is made of cane. Our hammocks are woven with thread made from palm leaves. And we often drink from gourds painted with bright flowers.

All these things were made far from our plantation in villages all over Brazil. Many of them were gifts from relatives. Brazilians have big families and we like to get together often.

Last Sunday was my birthday and I had a wonderful party. Counting my aunts and uncles and all my cousins, more than thirty people came.

For lunch my mother cooked rice, beans, onions, smoked sausage, bacon, and the tongue, feet, ears, and tail of a pig. For dessert we had bowls of ice cream and a huge frosted cake with candles.

Then my sister Telma played her guitar, my cousin Roberto played the piano, and I tried my new accordion. Antonio's pet monkey danced on the piano as long as the music lasted.

In the evening after all the guests went home we watched television. My father chooses westerns, but I like programs about children in other countries. It would be fun to visit all those places. Maybe someday I can come to see you. I hope so very much.

Chen-fu from China

Water Buffalo

Grain Mill

Tung-kua Melons

I have three brothers—Cheng, Chang, and Chiang—and my name is Chen-fu. Can you guess where you are? If you say China, you are right.

We live on a farm near the village of Ch'u. The courtyard outside our house is noisy with animals. I feed our squealy pigs and my brothers look after the chickens, geese, and ducks. My sister Hsu takes care of our burro and water buffalo.

A water buffalo works hard on a Chinese farm. Ours pulls a wooden plow so that we can plant our crops of rice and corn.

Our burro works hard too. She turns the grain mill in our courtyard to grind our corn into meal.

Today we're going to market to sell the tung-kua melons we grow in our garden. My father hitches our water buffalo to a heavy wooden cart, and we ride down the road and through the huge gate into the village.

Ch'u is a busy, exciting place filled with people. Dogs run through the crowd, barking and chasing one another. At the market everyone seems to be shouting at once. "Buy my baskets!" "Buy my hats!" "Buy my mats!" We find a place to unload our cart and then my father shouts too: "Buy my melons!"

When my brothers and I are not needed to help, we find other boys our age and go play. Our favorite game is called Fighting Cock. To play this game, we hop on one leg and try to push each other over. Chiang is the best Fighting Cock in our family, but sometimes I win.

After market we return home, and soon good smells come from my mother's stove. Tonight she is preparing *chung-tze,* a dish made of meat and rice. With it we will drink green tea from small cups. Sometimes she cooks noodles. But what I like best are her dumplings, which are as big as oranges.

When we eat, we will sit on low stools at a wooden table. If you have never used chopsticks, I'll show you how. With your left hand hold the bowl close to your mouth, and use the chopsticks with your right hand to pick up your food. Don't worry if you spill some. Our puppy will thank you for it!

After supper is the best time of day. Chiang sits in the courtyard and plays tunes on his *erh hu,* which looks something like a fiddle. Our father takes us for rides on the burro or sits and tells us stories. Our mother listens while she sews.

When the sun goes down, it's time to go in. My house has one main room with plaster walls, a brick floor, and wooden beams in the ceiling. Along one wall is a wide shelf called the *kang.* During the day we sit there to work or talk. At night we cover the *kang* with mats and it becomes our bed.

It has been a good day and I feel happy. The next time you come maybe my mother will fix us some of her big dumplings.

Cover for Cooking Well

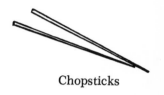

Chopsticks

Table and Stools

Chiang's *Erh Hu*
and Bow to Play It

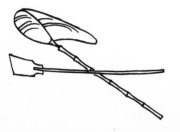

Flyswatter
and Insect Net

Robin from the United States

Robin's Bulletin Board

Record Player

Clock

My name is Robin, and I live in Kansas City, Missouri, in a one-story house on a street lined with shady, green elm trees.

Would you like to see my bedroom? It has two tall windows so I can look out into the backyard. And it has a desk with a lamp and a bookcase that I helped my mother paint. Beside my bed is a little round rug for my feet on chilly winter mornings. On the wall is a bulletin board. I pin papers and pictures on it that I don't want to lose.

Each morning after our milk and cereal, my brother Jeff and I make our beds and help clean the house. We carry out the papers and dust the tables and chairs in the family room, living room, and dining room. Sometimes we go with our mother to shop for groceries. After that we're ready for fun.

Do you like to swim? During the summer we go to the swimming pool nearly every day. Many of our friends go there too so we all keep cool together. On other days we play softball or ride our bicycles or listen to records.

Best of all I like camping. On warm weekends my father hooks our camper to the car, and we drive fifty miles to a lake. It's pretty there. We see squirrels and chipmunks and wild flowers and many kinds of butterflies and birds.

Coffeepot

Grill for Cooking

Ice Chest

Forks for Cooking Meat
on Grill

We cook out and ride horseback and swim and take long hikes in the woods. Usually my father rents a boat and we go fishing. Jeff and I always have a contest to see who catches the biggest fish.

Last weekend Jeff brought home a can full of tadpoles. Now he's trying to raise them in our goldfish bowl. We also have a cat named Whiskers and a parakeet named Tony. Tony lives inside a cage and wishes he could get out. Whiskers lives outside the cage and wishes she could get in.

When my father comes home from the office in the evening, he likes to work in the yard. Sometimes Jeff and I help him pull weeds or water the flowers. Often he lights the charcoal grill and barbecues meat for our dinner. Then we eat outside on our patio.

Popcorn

Goldfish and Tadpoles

After dinner I practice my piano lessons. Then I watch television or look at books. Near bedtime Jeff and I like to pop a bowlful of hot buttered popcorn. Before I go to sleep my mother or father may come into my room and read me a story. My favorite is about a spider named Charlotte who saves a pig named Wilbur.

The last thing I heard last night was Jeff getting out of bed. He had forgotten to feed his tadpoles. I hope he remembers tonight.

I'm very glad you came to see me today. Please come back soon.

Mendak from India

Water Jars

Camel Bells

My name is Mendak, and I live in a village in India. I'm glad this isn't the rainy season. Then heavy clouds pour big, long drops that burst like glass straws on our courtyard. Everything turns to mud and it is no fun to be outdoors.

But now it's the dry season, and the dust on the road is ankle-deep and as soft as flour. Every day after breakfast I build dust castles in it with my brother Bagha. Village women with brass water jars on their heads go by on their way to the well.

Other people pass along the road too. On festival days camel drivers ride by, taking their animals to the city for the camel races. Once I saw a man with a bear trained to dance if you gave its master a few coins.

Sometimes we see men riding wrinkle-skinned elephants to work in railroad yards. They use the huge beasts to push heavy boxcars into place.

When Bagha and I feel hot and dusty, we cool off in the river. Silvery chital fish play around us, but they're too fast to catch with our hands.

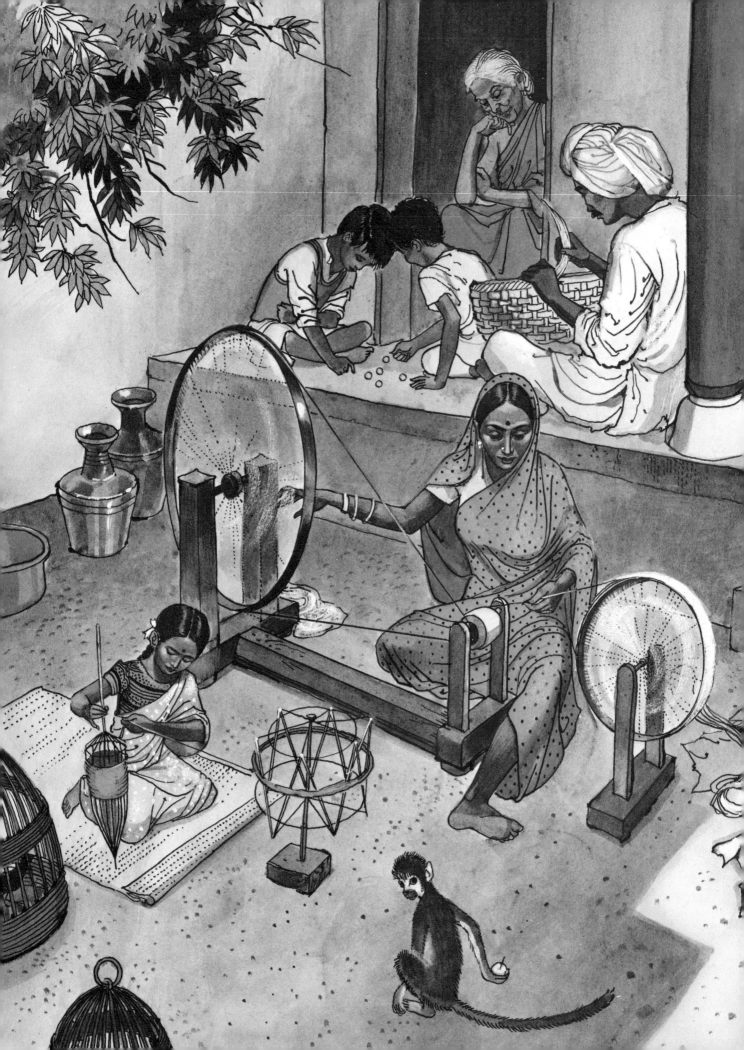

At noon our father comes home from his shop in the village, where he sells bamboo mats and baskets. For lunch we have bread and rice with a vegetable such as eggplant. We may also have bananas no bigger then your fingers or mangoes or figs.

Father's Baskets and a Mat

We eat with our right hand and use pieces of bread to scoop up the rice. My favorite dessert is candy made by boiling milk until it turns as thick as fudge.

In the hot afternoons we rest in the shade of our courtyard. My father weaves more baskets and mats for his shop. My sister Deepali helps my mother spin thread into cloth for clothes.

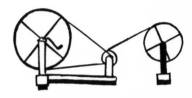

Spinning Wheel and Reel

Bagha and I shoot marbles or play Hide-and-Seek or play with our pets. This summer we caught a baby monkey in some trees near our house, and Deepali caught a myna bird.

We are outdoors so much that we don't need a large house. The walls and floor are made of mud that has dried as hard as wood. The roof is tile. Our kitchen has a mud stove and large pottery jars for storing food. Wooden bowls, brass dishes, and metal cooking pans line the shelves.

Charpoy

We sleep in the other room on wooden beds called *charpoys*. On hot nights we carry our *charpoys* outside where it is cooler. Then we can watch large fruit-eating bats leave their roosts in banyan trees and swoop off through the air as darkness falls.

In the morning, before daylight, I'll be awakened by the squawking of wild peacocks and the cawing of crows. My mother's bracelets will jingle as she moves about the kitchen. Then my father will cough and recite his morning prayers to let all the family know that a new day has come to India.

Peacocks

Rifa'a from Saudi Arabia

Bedouin Woman's Dress

Leather Water Bag

Would you like to ride a camel? You can if you stay with me. I'm Rifa'a. My people are Bedouins, and we live in Saudi Arabia on a great desert of rolling sand. Our strong camels carry us and our belongings as we move from one camp to another.

Let me show you our tent. I'm proud of it because I helped my mother make it. We spun sheep's wool into thread with our spindle and then wove the thread into strips of cloth with our loom. With long goat-hair thread, we sewed the strips together and used them to make our tent.

I also help set up the tent because that is the women's task. My young brothers, Emir and Jabr, help too, but they will not when they are older. Their job is to pound into the ground the pegs that hold the tent-pole ropes.

While we women finish the tent, the boys cut firewood from an 'arfaj bush and fill our leather water bags at the well.

53

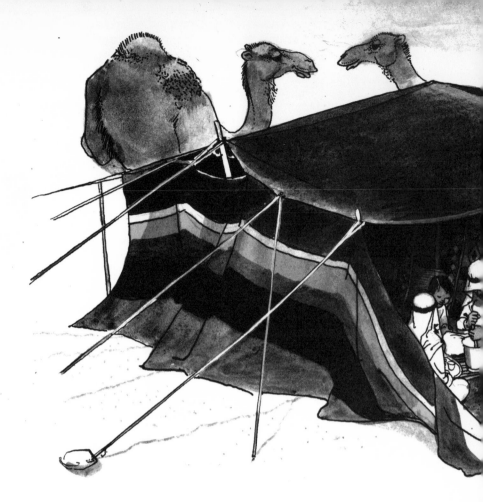

Spindle and Sheep's Wool

Brass Bowl for
Grinding Coffee Beans

Coffeepot, Cups,
and Bowl of Camel's Milk

Our tent has three rooms. At one end is the men's quarters. There the ground is covered by a carpet, and there are mattresses and cushions to sit on. In the middle of the room is a small fireplace. Nearby my father keeps three coffeepots, which have long pointed spouts, and a brass case filled with tiny china cups. He also sets out the coffee-bean roaster, the brass bowl for grinding the beans, and the wooden peg for stirring the coffee. Serving coffee to guests is a very important custom among Bedouins.

The center room is the women's quarters. Here I set out our spindle and loom. My mother hangs our camel saddlebags on tent poles and stacks our heavy red sleeping quilts on bags of flour, rice, sugar, salt, and dates.

The last room is our kitchen. Here we dig a hole for the cooking fire and set out the pots and pans. A large stack of 'arfaj firewood fills one corner.

54

Tonight for supper there will be lamb cooked with rice. Afterward we will eat fresh dates and drink cool camel milk from large bowls. When I eat I will kneel on my left knee, sit on my heel, and pick up my food with the fingers of my right hand.

I will feed the leftover scraps to our four dogs. Two are pets that sleep inside the tent with us. They are good hunters and my father takes them along when he hunts gazelle and desert hares.

The other two are big shaggy watchdogs that prowl in circles around the tent at night. They protect our camels and sheep from the wolves that hunt in the desert during the dark hours.

Now it is night and time to close our tent until tomorrow. I'm sorry you couldn't stay longer. Please come back soon. Until we meet again, as we say in the desert, "Peace be upon you!"

Rug for Sandy Floor of Tent

Leather Pillow to Lean On

Ian from Australia

Kangaroo

Water Tank and
Windmill to Pump Water

I am Ian, and I'm glad you've come to visit. Our next-door neighbors live ten miles away, so we don't have company often.

My family lives in Australia on a cattle and sheep ranch, called a station. The best thing about living on a station is being around so many animals. My little sister Anne is raising a lamb, and I have a calf that will soon be big enough to carry Anne on its back.

We have a pony too, and nearly every day we brush his mane and tail until they shine. Then we ride him around the barnyard. Our three border collies have been trained to herd sheep. One just had five puppies, which we're keeping in a box on the porch.

Wild kangaroos live all over our station. I have a tame one, named Peter, that sleeps in the barn. Each morning when I yell, "Hey, Peter!" he hops across the yard to the kitchen door to have his ears scratched.

Besides taking care of my calf and the puppies, I feed the chickens, gather eggs, and help my father milk the cows. Anne pulls weeds in the vegetable garden and dusts the furniture.

Two-Way Radio
and Microphone

Dingoes

Brumbies

The part of Australia where we live is called the Outback. It's so huge that people often travel by airplane. Last year when I was sick, my father used the two-way radio in our living room to call a doctor 100 miles away. Before long, the doctor landed his plane near our house and walked into my room.

We have a plane too. I love flying over the station with my father to check the stock. Coming home, we buzz low over the landing strip to chase away the cows and kangaroos grazing on the grass.

Our house is built to help us keep cool in the hot Outback country. It has wooden floors, high ceilings, and tall windows that catch the breezes. Through the center of the house runs a wide hall. Across the front is a closed-in porch. My room is at the back near the kitchen. On the mornings that my mother bakes bread the smell floats into my room and I wake up hungry.

Sometimes on Sunday afternoons my mother packs a big food basket. We saddle our horses and ride out to find a picnic spot with a shady tree. Many trees in Australia have funny names like cooba, gidgee, wait-awhile, and raspberry jamwood.

In the evenings I like to work on model planes. My desk and dresser are covered with my collection. Sometimes my father shows us movies or reads us stories. My favorite ones are about dingoes and brumbies. Dingoes are wild dogs that roam in the Outback. Brumbies are wild horses. I've seen herds of them from the plane.

Bedtime comes early at our station because we get up early in the morning. Thank you for stopping. I hope sometime soon you can come to the Outback again.

Children Everywhere

Tonight children everywhere will go to sleep. Some will snuggle in soft beds under fresh-smelling sheets and warm blankets. Others will curl up on wooden shelves. Some will lie on the ground. Their houses may be built of mud or snow or wood or animal skins or brick or grass. For dinner they may have eaten roots or coconuts or rice or fish or hamburgers or nothing at all.

During bitter winter nights, Utak's snow house becomes so cold that he sleeps in his fur clothes to stay warm. But he can dream of hunting seals with his father and skimming across the ice on a dogsled the way Eskimos have always done.

Rain may pour through the top of Martta's tent and drench everything her family owns. But she thinks it's nice to milk her own reindeer and sing old Lapp songs as her mother bakes fish pies.

Toma sometimes goes to bed with an empty stomach. But he can lie watching the stars and listening to the night sounds of Africa as his people have done for a long time.

Boys and girls around the world grow up in different ways. But no matter how they live or where they live, children in every land love their families and feel proud of the traditions of their people. Home everywhere can be a good place to be.

And that's nice to think about!